Derby

IN OLD PHOTOGRAPHS

Arnold and Dorothy Eley of Riddings Street on their wedding day in 1921.

Derby

IN OLD PHOTOGRAPHS

Collected by DAVID BUXTON

In collaboration with
Derbyshire County Council

Alan Sutton Publishing Limited
Phoenix Mill · Far Thrupp · Stroud
Gloucestershire · GL5 2BU

First published in 1992
Reprinted 1994, 1996

British Library Cataloguing in Publication Data.
Buxton, David
Derby in Old Photographs
I. Title
942.517

ISBN 0–7509–0273–6

Typeset in 9/10 Sabon.
Typesetting and origination by
Alan Sutton Publishing Limited.
Printed in Great Britain by
WBC Limited, Bridgend.

Office workers at Rolls-Royce's new factory in Nightingale Road, *c.* 1910.

Contents

Introduction   7

1. The Market Place and the Corn Market   9

2. Industry   29

3. London Road   53

4. Sports and Leisure   59

5. The Morledge and Cockpit Hill   83

6. Road Transport   93

7. Shops and Trades   113

8. St Peter's Street, Victoria Street and The Wardwick   123

9. Iron Gate and Sadler Gate   135

10. Railways   143

11. The Derby Ram   158

    Acknowledgements   160

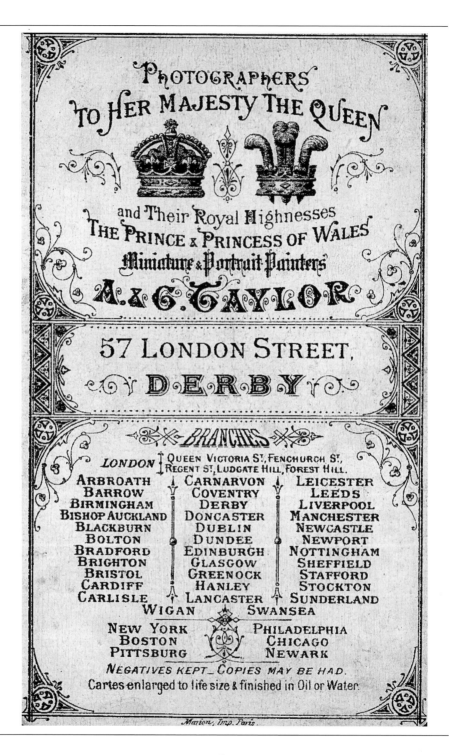

PHOTOGRAPHERS
TO HER MAJESTY THE QUEEN

and Their Royal Highnesses
THE PRINCE & PRINCESS OF WALES
Miniature & Portrait Painters
A. & G. TAYLOR

57 LONDON STREET,
DERBY

BRANCHES

LONDON ⎰ QUEEN VICTORIA ST., FENCHURCH ST.,
⎱ REGENT ST., LUDGATE HILL, FOREST HILL.

ARBROATH	CARNARVON	LEICESTER
BARROW	COVENTRY	LEEDS
BIRMINGHAM	DERBY	LIVERPOOL
BISHOP AUCKLAND	DONCASTER	MANCHESTER
BLACKBURN	DUBLIN	NEWCASTLE
BOLTON	DUNDEE	NEWPORT
BRADFORD	EDINBURGH	NOTTINGHAM
BRIGHTON	GLASGOW	SHEFFIELD
BRISTOL	GREENOCK	STAFFORD
CARDIFF	HANLEY	STOCKTON
CARLISLE	LANCASTER	SUNDERLAND

WIGAN   SWANSEA

NEW YORK	PHILADELPHIA
BOSTON	CHICAGO
PITTSBURG	NEWARK

NEGATIVES KEPT_ COPIES MAY BE HAD.
Cartes enlarged to life size & finished in Oil or Water.

Marion, Imp. Paris.

Introduction

This book does not attempt to tell the history of Derby. Rather, it is a haphazard collection of images gathered from libraries and museums, company files, newspaper offices and family albums; photographs taken at different times and for different reasons, with a variety of aims and motives, and none of them taken with a history book in mind. And yet, gathered together, they provide an intriguing and informative, sometimes even amusing, window on the social life of Derby over a period of about a hundred years, from the 1860s to the 1960s.

Most of the earliest photographs of Derby that we know of were taken in the 1860s by Richard Keene. A pioneer local photographer, he had an eye for a good picture as well as an instinct for recording that which was about to change. His records of the alterations to Iron Gate and the Market Place of this period, for example, are invaluable. Following the arrival of the railway in town in the 1840s, and the increase in industrialization and traffic that followed, Derby began to feel the need to modernize its streets. A series of street-widening programmes was initiated and new buildings of a type more appropriate to a town now on the industrial map began to appear.

The initiative to make improvements came from the business community, often an individual, rather than the town council. Today we are more used to the 'drive to modernize' arising from policy moves made in town and county halls, sometimes by committees that lack any 'feel' for the town. Derby has surely suffered greatly in this way in recent decades.

The move to widen Iron Gate and to demolish the Shambles came, in each case, from an individual setting up a subscription fund to raise cash to compensate the displaced and effect the reconstruction. A Derby shopkeeper, Henry Steer, who had set up the fund to raze the Shambles, wrote in a letter to the *Derby Mercury* in October 1891, that he was opening up a subscription list at the Derby and Derbyshire Bank to finance the widening of Sadler Gate. This too was eventually done.

The mid- and late nineteenth century in Derby saw some enlightened improvements to the recreational, cultural and health facilities as well as street alterations. Derby's altruistic MP of many years, Sir Michael Bass, provided recreation grounds, swimming baths, and the library and museum complex, while Joseph Strutt donated eleven acres of land near Osmaston Road as a 'pleasure garden', landscaped by Loudon and called the Arboretum. This gift to the town was the first example of a public park in the country. In the 1890s more public subscription provided for the building of a new hospital, opened by Queen Victoria as the Derbyshire Royal Infirmary.

The new century saw the arrival of new industries and the further growth of Derby as a centre for engineering expertise, enhanced when the young Rolls and Royce built their factory here. Pictures of their early years in Derby provide a record that is of international interest.

The photographic record of Derby's 'lost buildings' is sometimes a sad one to contemplate. Even in these times of supposed conservation awareness, and at a time when there is an unprecedented growth in the study of local history, it is still possible to 'justify' the demolition of commercially inconvenient buildings. This is not a new phenomenon and is probably one that will always prevail so long as business takes precedence over aesthetics. But this strikes too gloomy a note. Derby possesses many good buildings and I hope that seeing some of them in the context of these old pictures will stimulate a renewed interest in those that are still available to be enjoyed. I hope too that all these scenes of Derby and Derby people over the years will bring back memories for some and enlighten others as to how the town used to be and what it still has to offer.

Trolley buses in the Market Place in the 1950s

SECTION ONE

The Market Place and the Corn Market

The Market Place on a wet evening in the late 1930s. The War Memorial was designed by C.A. Thompson and erected in 1924. Its unusual style was not universally welcomed when it was first put up and there had been alternative proposals. One of these was to build a new riverside garden by Derwent Bridge as a more utilitarian memorial.

Rotten Row. In the late 1860s some alterations were made to the town centre that dramatically changed the appearance and use of a corner of the Market Place. Rotten Row was opened up when a large block of shops known as the Shambles (right) was demolished, along with its later addition, the Piazzas. The narrow street that was formed between the Shambles and Market Head (left) led from the south side of the Market Place, in the foreground, to Iron Gate (as yet unwidened), in the rear of the picture, and was known as Rotten Row.

The Market Place side of the Piazzas, *c.* 1869. Demolition of the northern side is under way.

The rear corner of the Shambles undergoing demolition in 1869. The view is from the end of Iron Gate looking into the Market Place; the opening to Sadler Gate is on the right.

The Piazzas, seen here from the Market Place side, *c.* 1869. This elegant forerunner of the modern shopping precinct was built in 1708 by the banker Abraham Crompton and had a covered walk in front of the shops. Crompton's piece of speculative building was an addition to the existing structure, purpose-built as butchers shops in the late seventeenth century and known as the Shambles. The northern end has been demolished.

A mustering of Volunteer Yeomanry in the Market Place in 1865. The Derbyshire Yeomanry Cavalry were revived in 1864 under Government order and this may be their first assembly.

The newly widened Market Place following complete removal of the Shambles and the Piazzas, *c.* 1877. The area was relaid with new cobbles and there was a firework display to celebrate the completion.

The west side of the Market Place in 1877. The centre building was Smith's Bank which has now disappeared. The building to its right (built in 1839) survives, although a little changed. Notice the entrance to Mason's tap house between the two of them.

A huge crowd has gathered to see the unveiling of a statue of Derby benefactor and MP, Sir Michael Bass, in 1885. A popular figure, he provided funds for recreation grounds, swimming baths, and the library and museum. The statue is now in The Wardwick.

The Market Place on market day in the 1890s. The Town Hall was rebuilt by Duesbury and Lee after a fire in 1841.

The Market Place, *c*. 1903. The old Assembly Rooms are visible on the left.

The Mayor's Parlour. This fine Tudor house in Tennant Street, just off the Market Place, was never actually used by the mayor as far as anyone knows. Having successfully survived bombing during the Second World War, it was demolished as part of an 'improvement scheme' in 1948.

A horse-drawn tram may be seen at the bottom of this photograph of the Market Place, *c*. 1900.

An electric tram now operates in the Market Place, *c*. 1910. There have been some changes to the buildings too.

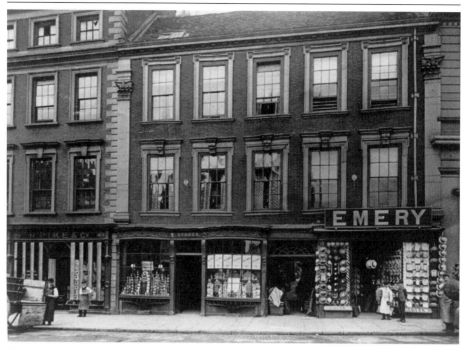

Shops on the west side of the Market Place, including Emery's, the hat dealers, *c*. 1900. This building was originally the home and business premises of the Storer family. It was later converted again by Austin and Co. (see opposite) and then demolished in 1936. A bank now stands on the site.

A busy market day, *c*. 1910.

Austin & Co., the grocers, occupied Storer's house here in 1920.

This market picture was taken in 1924, the year that the new Barlow and Taylor's building was constructed. Scaffolding surrounding the construction can be seen in the background.

The new Barlow and Taylor's building, finished in 1925, now dominates the corner of Iron Gate and the Market Place.

A familiar view of the Market Place and the War Memorial from under the archway of the Guildhall, *c.* 1924. For many years this draughty thoroughfare was the sales pitch for Monk's excellent pikelets and oatcakes.

Barlow and Taylor's corner following road widening in the early 1930s.

Cope and Taylor's shop in 1935. The elegant fittings in this shop dated from the middle of the last century, and the use of the premises as an apothecary's went back to 1646 when Henry Francey built the house. Cope and Taylor's closed in 1971.

The Assembly Rooms, built by Joseph Pickford in 1763, are seen here in 1931. Ramsden's restaurant on the right provided catering services for functions at the Assembly Rooms, although the Horse and Trumpet in Full Street did so at other times. The building was severely damaged by a fire and, after much deliberation, it was decided to demolish rather than restore it. It came down in 1963 to be replaced by the unsympathetic and oversized modern version that now unfortunately dominates the area that used to be the Market Place.

Derwent Street and Tennant Street junction which formed the south-east corner of the Market Place. This building has been demolished and schemes to build something new on the site have all failed. At the time of writing the area is an abandoned construction site.

The Market Place in the early 1960s.

A scene outside Austin's in the Market Place as the great flood of 1932 subsides and people, probably much relieved, start to treat it as a joke.

The Corn Market from the Market Place in 1865. This picture predates the widening of St James' Lane to make St James' Street. It appears that the necessary demolition of the two buildings on the right, just before the lane, may already have begun.

The floods of 1932 submerged the Corn Market under several feet of water. Note the crowd of onlookers in Victoria Street.

The Corn Market, facing the Market Place, in 1924. In winter the policeman on point duty at the junction with St James' Street was provided with straw to stand on to keep his feet warm.

Industry

In the early years of the century an enterprising young man who served as secretary to the Derby Borough Development Committee was responsible, through his zeal, for bringing to the town several important new industries that helped shape its modern history. By promoting Derby's virtues as an industrial centre, he succeeded in attracting several important new engineering companies seeking new sites for expansion. One of these was none other than Rolls-Royce. Another was Aiton and Co. Arthur Aiton, engineer and pipe manufacturer, moved from London to Stores Road in Derby in 1907. The company grew rapidly, making specialist steam-pipes for ships and power stations. Arthur Aiton (with a beard) is seen here in 1922 at the commissioning of a new corrugating machine, the rights to which he had just acquired from Pole Waclaw Kossowski (left). Corrugated pipes went round corners more easily than smooth ones, which was an important advantage in the 1920s .

A new steam separator built by Aiton's in 1925.

Sir Arthur Aiton explains the operation of a Bonn pipe-bending machine to visitors in 1931.

Aiton and Co. made headlines in 1931 when they commissioned new offices at Stores Road (above). The architects of this modern building were two young women, Betty Scott and Aiton's daughter, Norah. The design was well ahead of its time, being built completely of concrete and steel with large areas of glass wall. The furniture included black lacquered desks and chromium-plated steel chairs, with floors covered in red lino.

Arthur Aiton was active in Derby's public affairs, and as chairman of the Chamber of Commerce hosted the visit of King George V and Queen Mary to the royal show in Derby in 1933. Looking remarkably like the King himself, he is seen here (wearing the black top hat) escorting the royal visitors past his own company's stand. Notice the corrugated pipe on show.

Workmen at the varnish factory of Joseph Mason and Co. Ltd at the Burton Road works in about 1890. This old firm began work in 1800 at a site close to the bridge in Derwent Street.

The trade stand of Joseph Mason and Co. Ltd on the same royal show occasion in 1933 as the one seen opposite. The company by this time had developed from varnish makers to manufacturers of a range of specialist paints for coach bodywork. This stand displayed a scale model of the Irish State Coach, the full-sized version of which was painted entirely with the company's materials. The company still occupy a site on the Nottingham Road first acquired in 1900. A Derby landmark from their Burton Road days was a tall chimney with a curiously shaped top, built to disperse paint and varnish fumes. The chimney was apparently notoriously ineffective and dubbed 'Mason's Folly'. It survived until 1962.

The Union Jack flies and a handful of people witness the comings and goings of a ceremony that was important in the history of the motor car. The event, at Nightingale Road
in 1908, was the opening of the new factory of Rolls-Royce Ltd. Inside the building were
key figures in the history of the industry: Henry Royce, brilliant designer and engineer,
and creator of the already famous 'Silver Ghost'; his new partner C.S. Rolls, whose sales
expertise had promoted the car; and Lord Montague, whose parliamentary activities had
enabled the growth of the 'motor age'. Prior to Montague's Act a red flag had preceded all
motor cars and speed limits had been unrealistically low.

The opening ceremony. Standing behind the silver cup is Lord Montague, making his speech. Seated third from his left is C.S. Rolls (with hand to his face), and to *his* right and almost obscured from view is Henry Royce. The man seated on the right, behind the lady in white, is Henry Edmunds who first introduced Rolls to Royce. On the lady's right is the company chairman, Ernest Claremont. Behind the group is the Silver Ghost car that had just completed a record-breaking 15,000 mile non-stop run.

The new factory site in Nightingale Road. The space in front of the factory, built on at a later date, was occupied by the marquees during the opening ceremony.

The new factory building was designed by Henry Royce. Initially, as an economy, the offices were housed in a part of the workshops separated by wood and glass partitions. The man standing to the right of centre is John de Looze, company secretary of F.H. Royce Ltd in 1893 who continued as secretary of Rolls-Royce Ltd (founded in 1906) until 1943.

A production line of Silver Ghosts at the new factory. Henry Royce produced several different models of car in the first few years but, because of its popularity, the Silver Ghost became the sole product for several years. From the earliest days the cars were famous for their reliability.

A group of workers at the factory posing in front of an array of signs. Royce's first factory had been in Manchester and most of the staff migrated south when the firm moved. Single men walked to Derby, but families were given assistance with transport for themselves and their belongings.

A view of the office, c. 1910. Company secretary John de Looze is standing in the centre talking to the commissionaire.

At the outbreak of the First World War the British Government asked Rolls-Royce to begin building a military aeroplane. The company was to fit Renault engines in aircraft of British design. Royce only agreed to do this on condition that, as soon as he had developed a suitable engine of his own, it would replace the foreign one. This was agreed, and he designed and built the Eagle engine from scratch to test stage (above) in six months. The Eagle engine was highly successful and eventually used to power forty-eight different aircraft, including airships.

The statue of Henry Royce, erected in 1923 by the company's shareholders and seen here in the Riverside Gardens. It was removed to the new Rolls-Royce works at Sinfin in 1988. Although the company is known world-wide as Rolls-Royce, in Derby it has always been referred to as 'Royces'.

Merlin Supercharger aero-engines under construction just before the Second World War. By the end of the war 150,000 of these engines had been built and used to power Spitfire, Hurricane, Mustang, Lancaster and Mosquito aircraft. Gas turbine research at Rolls-Royce in 1938, in co-operation with Frank Whittle, led to the production, by 1943, of the first successful jet engines which were used to power Meteor jets.

Workers leaving the factory in the 1940s. Car production in Derby stopped in 1940 and transferred to Crewe, but aero-engine research and production continues at the Sinfin works to this day.

The Derby Crown Porcelain Company – a print of the new works in Osmaston Road, probably made around the time of its opening in 1877. The factory continued a tradition of fine porcelain manufacture in Derby that began when Andrew Planche opened a workshop in 1750.

A scene in a workshop at the old factory in Kings Road, *c.* 1935. The wheel in use in this picture is said to be the same one used two hundred years earlier by William Duesbury, owner of the earlier Nottingham Road factory.

In 1890 the company was appointed 'Manufacturer of Porcelain to Her Majesty' and was renamed Royal Crown Derby. Mr H.T. Robinson, chairman in 1937, is seen here holding a pair of china models.

The following group of photographs was commissioned in 1954 as part of a British crafts-people at work promotion. This picture shows Betty Consterdine and Mary Woodcock in the 'biscuit' room, checking china before firing.

Raymond Kirk modelling china figures.

The final check. Joyce Ford and Hazel Foxon inspect china before packing it for despatch.

Clara Smart (right) had worked for Royal Crown Derby for fifty-four years when this photograph was taken in 1954. She was an expert at applying decoration to china and here watches Jean Lowe burnishing a gold line onto a dinner plate with bloodstone.

Derby's long association with the textile industry began with silk-spinning in the late eighteenth century, and a variety of mills has come and gone since those pioneering days. Here are the owners of Lilley's Tape Mills in Dean Street. Mr Lilley is wearing a bowler hat and his wife is sitting in front of him, *c.* 1900.

Moore and Eddie's Mill in Markeaton Street, seen here in the early years of the century, still operates today as a clothing factory and shop.

The offices of Ley's Foundry in Colombo Street, seen here in the 1920s. The firm was established in 1874. It was after a visit to America in 1889 that the founder, Sir Francis Ley, was inspired to try to introduce baseball into Britain. He converted the firm's sports field into a baseball ground and encouraged several local football teams to compete. The venture was not a lasting success, but when the ground later became Derby County's home ground the name stuck.

This aerial view of Derby in 1928 clearly shows how much heavy industry there was in the heart of the city. In the centre, fronting onto Full Street, is the power station, only a narrow street's width from the rear of the Cathedral – a perennial bone of contention. There were three stages in the construction of the power station. The original building of 1892 quickly struggled to cope with the sudden growth in demand for electricity. A new, larger building replaced the former in 1908 (left). In 1920 another building was added (centre), sadly replacing the elegant Devonshire Hospital which was demolished to make room for it. The Silk Mill's distinctive tower can be seen next to the smoking chimney, and Full Street Baths and All Saints' Vicarage are visible on the extreme right. The power station was finally demolished in 1970 and the site grassed over.

The Shot Tower of Cox's Lead Works in the Morledge was a familiar landmark in the city. Built in 1809 by Messrs Cox and Poyser, it was 180 ft high and used for making lead shot. Lead was melted at the top of the tower and poured through a pan perforated with holes. The molten lead fell in droplets into a tank of water at the bottom. The tower caught fire in 1824 and was almost destroyed. When it was demolished in 1932, probably the year of this photograph, the crenellated top portion was purchased by Mr Dallman of Melbourne who used it as a garden ornament.

John Smith's shop and works in Queen Street, *c.* 1900. The firm, which made tower clocks for major buildings world-wide, was established in 1856 and grew rapidly. In 1893 a new clock was made for St Paul's which is still maintained by the company.

Smith and Sons' main workshop in 1936. Left to right: G. Hurd, L. Dainty, R. Policott, L. Shaw, Chris Newton, L. Jepson, E. Buckland, Harry Farnsworth, H. Lane, Billy Hurd, William Hurd (sen.).

Queen Street and St Alkmund's church in 1912. St Michael's church is just visible on the right, and Smith and Sons' premises are on the left. Smiths have maintained the clocks on most of Derby's churches over the years, including St Alkmund's (see opposite).

Bert Sherwood in 1958, working on a hand-wind clock destined for the West Indies.

A stunning view taken through the clock aperture of St Alkmund's church tower when repairs were being carried out on the clock in 1950. Jim Lee swings on a wooden seat high over the road to make the repairs, and there is a tantalizing glimpse of old Queen Street as it was before the ring road swept away the church and Bridge Gate in the late 1960s.

Loading a packed clock, bound for the University of Kansas, at Smiths in 1953. Left to right: Norman (British Railway's driver), Harry Morris, Peter Dawkins (behind), Billy Hurd, Eric Ladds.

George Noakes carrying out repairs at Smiths in 1958.

SECTION THREE
London Road

London Road, *c.* 1935. Derbyshire-born Florence Nightingale is commemorated outside the Derbyshire Royal Infirmary by a statue. Her advice was sought on the design of the Nightingale Wing which was built as an extension to the old building.

London Road looking south, *c.* 1913. Derbyshire Royal Infirmary is on the right behind the trees and the Congregational chapel, known as 'The Temple', is on the left.

The gates to the infirmary, London Road, with St Andrew's church in the background, *c.* 1910.

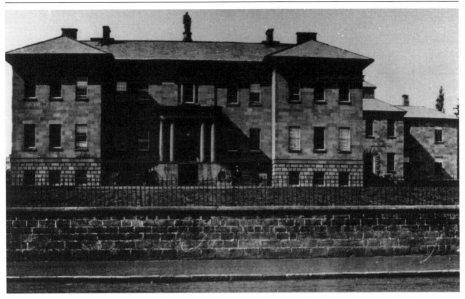

The Derbyshire Infirmary. Built in 1806–10 by William Strutt and Samuel Brown, the infirmary was modified by H.I. Stevens in 1869 to include a basement. By the 1890s it had become something of a scandal – it was unhygenic, difficult to clean and badly lit. It was demolished in 1896.

The new infirmary building by Young and Hall, as it appeared soon after completion, *c*. 1898.

Traffic Street leading down from London Road to Cockpit Hill, as it looked in 1937.

London Road looking north towards The Spot and the town centre, c. 1910.

The Prince of Wales and the Telegraph Inn on London Road by the junction with Traffic Street in 1920.

St Andrew's church, London Road, facing towards the centre of Derby. Holy Trinity church, which is opposite the infirmary, can be seen in the background. St Andrew's was demolished in 1972.

The Congregational chapel on the corner of London Road and Traffic Street was built by Derby architect H.I. Stevens in 1843. It closed as a chapel in the 1930s and, after suitable alterations, reopened as the Coliseum cinema. This picture was probably taken soon after the reopening. It was demolished in 1961 to clear a path for the new ring road.

SECTION FOUR
Sports and Leisure

Boys from Derby School rowing on the River Derwent in the 1930s.

An entrance gate to the Arboretum, a landscaped park given to the people of Derby in 1840 by Joseph Strutt and possibly the earliest public park in the country.

Like most children in Derby, Raymond and Peggy Buxton were regular visitors to the Arboretum. This studio portrait of about 1925 was taken by Winters of Midland Road.

This Italian marble statue of a boar was donated to the park by its founder, Joseph Strutt, and was a popular feature for children who were regularly photographed sitting on it. It was apparently destroyed by shrapnel from a bomb during the war.

The fountain made in 1841 for the Arboretum by the Derby firm of Handyside and Co.

Barbara Harrison was photographed wearing her best bow and boots at a photographic studio in Normanton Road in 1924.

Alvaston Lake was a popular spot for boating – and fishing too. Barbara Harrison remembers that in the 1920s they would dry off their fishing-nets on the way home from the lake by waving them out of the window on the top deck of the tram.

The Bridge Inn on Mansfield Road had its own landing-stage and boats for hire in the early years of the century.

Reginald Street Baths were opened in 1903, adding to several others already available in the town. Swimming was deemed a healthy activity, but slipper baths were also an important provision when many houses were without a bathroom. A former pupil at nearby Pear Tree School remembers that no breakfast was allowed on swimming days!

Full Street Baths, built in 1852 and demolished in 1929.

Derby County, a founder member of the Football League, was formed in 1884. This picture of 1935 shows Derby scoring from a classic header against Wolverhampton Wanderers at the Baseball Ground.

Alderman Laurie kicks off a ladies football match at the Baseball Ground in aid of the Mayor's Hospital Fund in 1927.

The girls of class two at Firs Estate School in Percy Street, *c.* 1922.

The Riverside Gardens in about 1935 before the building of the Council House in Corporation Street. Notice the bronze turtle on the plinth in the pond, one of a pair that was moved to Allestree Park when the gardens were reorganized.

Following the First World War, several schemes were discussed for a suitable memorial to Derby's war dead, a statue in the Market Place eventually being chosen. One enlightened scheme that was proposed, but not taken up, was the riverside garden, shown here in a drawing. The scheme had the attraction of tidying up the river banks as well as providing a lasting memorial.

This series of photographs taken in
1934–5 shows some of the stages in the
creation of the Riverside Gardens some ten
years after a similar scheme was proposed
as a memorial to the war dead.

This attractive view of the Derwent from the bridge in about 1860 has several landmarks to spot, from the tower of All Saints on the left to that of the Silk Mill on the right.

Derwent Street and Exeter Bridge undergoing widening and reconstruction in 1931.

The Council House and Riverside Gardens in 1965. The power station and Silk Mill can be seen in the background.

Children playing in Ha'penny Lane. The location is something of a mystery but it is believed to have been a small lane without houses, hence its absence from old street directories, adjoining Penny Long Lane.

Children enjoying a dray ride at the Mount Street chapel Sunday School treat, Whitsuntide 1922.

Frances and Leslie Wild, aged seven and six years, in 1915. They lived in Cummings Street.

Joyce Harrison, aged five, in her Aunt Alice's garden in 1920.

Boating on the River Derwent in 1929.

Children playing by the canal locks near the Nottingham Road.

The Becket Street Methodist church cricket team, *c.* 1933. Is it television that is responsible for the reduced interest today in outdoor activities like cricket and football? Back
row, left to right: -?-, Alf Camp, Martin Harrison, Chuck Poole, George Gee. Front row:
Arthur Osborne, Bine Payne, Norman Varney, Arthur Foster, Frank Osborne, -?-.

Rugby did not achieve mass support until much later than football, and here, in 1935,
Derby Rugby Football Club is playing a match on the municipal sports ground rather
than on a ground of its own.

Derby Lifeboat Day procession in about 1905.

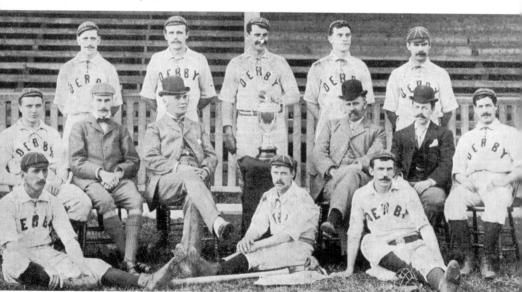

Winners of the English Baseball Cup in 1897. Francis Ley's team at the Baseball Ground was comprised mainly of Derby County players. Back row, left to right: D. Allsop, J. Evans, J. Reidenbach, J.W Robinson, E. Booth. Middle row: S. Bloomer, H.G. Ley, F. Ley, H.M. Gray, A. Langlands, T. Prestbury. Front row: J. Mellors, J. Saxton, W. Beresford.

May Day pageant in 1932 at the Practising School attached to the Training College in Uttoxeter Road. The 'Elizabethan' costumes were made in needlework classes and a May Queen was crowned. Back row, left to right: Nellie Alvey, Hilda Tunstall, Florrie Cadman, Irene Dickenson, Lily Bakewell, Barbara Harrison, Vera Guest. Middle row: Kathleen Sayles, Gwyneth Taylor, Doris Johnson. Front row: Edith Swift, Kathleen Rowlinson, Olive Bonshot, Doris Dickenson, Nancy Taylor, Mary Baker, Frances Hopton, Dorothy Kesterton.

A Sunday school procession in Dairy House Road in around 1905.

The unveiling of a statue of Queen Victoria at The Spot in 1906 by King Edward VII. The statue was later moved to the grounds of the Infirmary.

Children attending the school for the deaf in Friar Gate in about 1905.

The view from Derwent Street along Corporation Street to the Morledge in the early 1950s.

The Morledge and Cockpit Hill

The bus station soon after opening in 1932.

A high view of the Morledge on market day in 1911 with the Shot Tower, Guildhall and Cathedral on the sky-line.

The warehouses and factory buildings in the photograph above appear opposite but with a different set of posters. The lower photograph shows a continuation of these buildings, heading towards the cattle market.

Cockpit Hill in 1931 only a short time before the building of the bus station on the area behind the market stalls.

The Morledge mortuary and horse-drawn mortuary van in 1909. All these buildings were demolished when the bus station was built.

At the point where Siddals Road led away from Cockpit Hill there was a tall building known as the ice-factory, just visible on the left. Before the days of home and business refrigeration this company produced ice in bulk, for sale. Like many others this building was lost when the ring road was built.

An aerial view of the cattle market and the north side of the town in 1921. Cockpit Hill was off this picture to the bottom left.

The cattle market in full swing. The market on this site opened in 1861 and was one of the first losses as the ring road swept across this area.

The circus comes to town and elephants and camels move across Cockpit Hill heading for Bass's Rec. where the circus would be held.

The Morledge was home to visiting fairs like this one photographed in 1913.

Cockpit Hill in 1930, before the bus station was built.

The beginning of the demolition of Cockpit Hill before the construction of the Eagle Centre in 1970. The half destroyed Canal Tavern still bears the advertisement for Kimberley Ale that was prominent on the building forty years before (above).

When the bus station was built in 1932 the open market was moved onto a 'permanent' site alongside; the roofs of the stalls can be seen beyond the bus station.

SECTION SIX

Road Transport

A tram passing 'Five Lamps' at the bottom of Duffield Road, *c.* 1918. In those days the junction was still illuminated by five lamps.

A choice of horse-drawn transport from trams to hansom cabs was on offer in the Market Place in the 1890s. If refreshments were required another choice had to be made as there were at least two ice-cream sellers doing business when this photograph was taken.

A horse-drawn tram makes its way up the Corn Market, *c.* 1900.

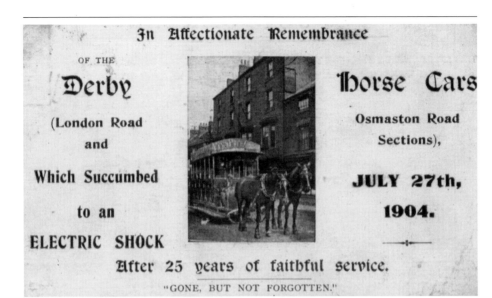

Horse-drawn trams operated in Derby from 1880. This humorous card, produced in 1904, commemorates the loss of only a part of the horse-drawn service to that of the electric tram. The final horse-drawn tram left Ashbourne Road for the centre of town in November 1907.

The tram terminus at Ashbourne Road in about 1900. Ashbourne Road Methodist church is in the background.

The first electric tram in Derby decorated for its maiden run in July 1904.

The Corn Market, *c*. 1906; a similar view to the one on page 94, but now horse power has given way to electric power for the tram. Hansom cabs, lined up for hire on the left, were common in Derby until about 1912.

The First World War revolutionized attitudes towards women and employment. With so many men at the front women did men's jobs for the first time. Bertha Harrison of Gerrard Street became a conductress on the trams although not, apparently, with the approval of her family.

Trams in Midland Road in about 1906. Midland Road was created in the 1840s after completion of the Midland station to give access to London Road.

Overcrowding on the last tram! A humorous card published in 1915 by printers J. Howard of Derby.

A tram on Normanton Road, *c.* 1905. Rose Hill Methodist church can be seen in the background.

The Nottingham Road as it passed under the Midland Railway bridge was lowered on one side to make room for trams, and later trolley buses, and their overhead power cables. After rain the hollow would fill with water.

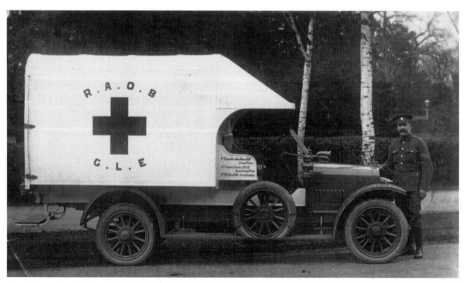

An elegantly-shaped ambulance belonging to the Royal Antediluvian Order of Buffaloes (The Derby Buffs) was seen in Derby during the First World War.

The Felix Bus Co. was founded in 1922 by Norman Frost, seen here on the left with Horace Sanders and Olga and Dora Frost in 1924. The bus is one of Frost's earliest; a Crossley lorry chassis with a Dickens coach body. The emblem on the front of the bus is Felix the Cat – a popular cartoon character at the time who has remained the emblem of the company. The company garage is still in the village of Stanley.

A Felix charabanc built on a Crossley chassis. Norman Frost is the driver for this early company excursion in 1922.

Another early Felix bus (*c.* 1926), this time a 30 cwt Dennis painted in maroon and red, colours that are still used on the modern coaches today.

This bus is a Bedford OB and was being used here in 1934 for the Derby to Ilkeston run, still a regular service by the company.

Another Bedford OB bus used by Felix seen at Derby bus station in 1953. After the war Felix acquired several buses from other companies which were not immediately painted in the company colours – this is one of them.

An outing for the Derby Butchers' Association to somewhere in Yorkshire, probably Scarborough, c. 1925.

Victoria Street at the junction with the Corn Market in about 1908. The Royal Hotel, Derby's Athenaeum, was built in 1840. The last trams left Victoria Street at 11 o'clock sharp each night. A tram inspector would stand in the middle of the road, blow his whistle and all the trams would depart together.

A works van belonging to John Smith and Sons passing along St Mary's Gate in 1952.

A battery-powered, electric motor parcel van used by Midland Railway in Derby, *c.* 1916.

A single-decker Trent bus picking up passengers at Derby bus station for an excursion to Alton Towers in the late 1930s.

A fine looking charabanc with solid tyres outside the Station Inn, Midland Road in 1920. The vehicle belonged to the Trent Motor Traction Co. and was driven by Mr F. Leigh of Belper whose father was landlord of the inn.

Two gentlemen in plus-fours choose their excursion on a Trent bus in the late 1930s. The Trent Motor Traction Co. was formed in 1913 and began with services to Ashbourne, Alfreton and Chesterfield. At the outbreak of the First World War the army commandeered nearly the whole fleet of buses.

A Trent bus at Derby bus station in the early 1940s. Notice the war-time headlamp covers for driving during black-outs.

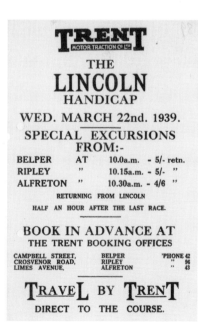

TRENT
MOTOR TRACTION Cº LTD

THE

LINCOLN
HANDICAP

WED. MARCH 22nd. 1939.

SPECIAL EXCURSIONS
FROM:-

BELPER	AT	10.0a.m.	- 5/- retn.
RIPLEY	"	10.15a.m.	- 5/- "
ALFRETON	"	10.30a.m.	- 4/6 "

RETURNING FROM LINCOLN

HALF AN HOUR AFTER THE LAST RACE.

BOOK IN ADVANCE AT
THE TRENT BOOKING OFFICES

CAMPBELL STREET,	BELPER	'PHONE 42
CROSVENOR ROAD,	RIPLEY	" 96
LIMES AVENUE,	ALFRETON	" 43

TRAVEL BY TRENT
DIRECT TO THE COURSE.

A Trent bus excursion poster of 1939.

These three pictures show old Trent buses decorated for the hospital carnival processions in the 1920s. Many Derby firms entered floats for this annual fund-raising event.

A lorry belonging to Joseph Mason Paints and displaying some of their range is about to take part in a celebration parade in 1954 for the 750th anniversary of the granting of a charter to the town by King John.

A Midland Railway electric parcel van used in Derby, *c.* 1921.

SECTION SEVEN

Shops and Trades

Arthur Harrison at the door of his butchers shop in Uttoxeter New Road, *c.* 1925.

An advertisement from a trade publication of 1935.

Battie's drapery shop in Sadler Gate in the early years of the century. The business continued in this shop for many years.

The so-called Lock Up Yard between the Market Hall and the Corn Market still survives as an area for fish and poultry stalls. Stringer's display in this picture of about 1920 includes an enormous fish and some rather less impressive poultry.

The sweet factory of White, Thomas and Sons in Full Street.

SUTTON-BUILT HOMES

are obtainable in all parts of Derby and Derbyshire

Specification includes

Extra deep
foundations

Steel Casements

Underfelting to
whole of roof and
Finest work-
manship throughout

*Specially low rent-
purchase terms
have been arranged*

or a house costing **£475** a deposit of **£25** and the balance at **12/6** per week, all costs include

ices of Houses and Bungalows range from **£399** to **£1,200** and upwards. Each place plann
specially. A portfolio of over 100 plans and suggestions. *Write for particulars*

T. H. SUTTON & SON, Builders
92a OSMASTON ROAD, DERBY   Telephone 3200

An advertisement from a trade journal of 1935.

Houses under construction in Osmaston Road in about 1935.

Underwear from Wolsey and Rameses is advertised on a building by Exeter Bridge.

The old Wholesale Market in Nottingham Road in the 1920s.

Jefferson's drapery shop at Albert House on the corner of the Corn Market and Albert Street, 1882.

Mr Allton the butcher with his apprentice boy at his shop in Normanton Road in about 1906.

Staff of the Ceylon Tea Warehouse in London Road in about 1954.

The Borough Council stables in Nottingham Road where the Council horses used for hauling refuse carts were housed. Also in this picture are Council steam traction-engines and steamrollers.

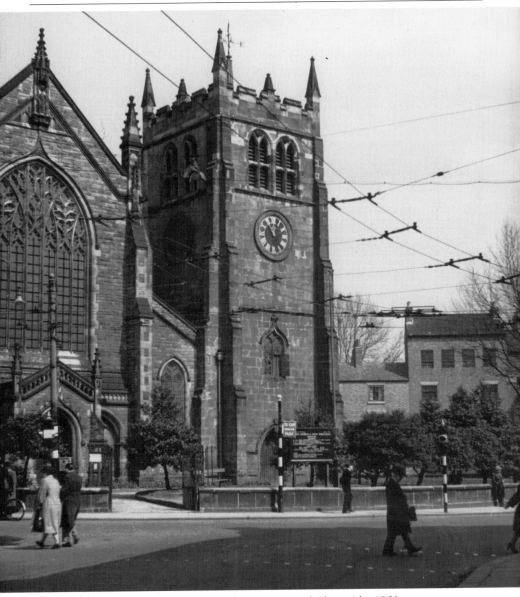

St Werburgh's church at the junction of Friar Gate and Cheapside, 1950.

St Peter's Street
Victoria Street
and The Wardwick

St Peter's Street from the Corn Market in about 1910.

The Wardwick in the early years of the century.

St Peter's Street looking north towards the Corn Market in about 1860. The basket-maker on the right was established in 1830 and was well known for inventing specialist baskets including a gamekeeper's arm shield and a wicker coffin.

The Wardwick from the clock tower of the library seen here in the late 1950s.

St Peter's Street shops leading up to St Peter's churchyard, in about 1881. The old gabled house next to the churchyard, known as Victoria House, was soon to be closed and demolished.

Victoria House closed following a compulsory sale in 1882.

The empty Victoria House soon collected a host of posters and it is possible also to see that the last occupiers moved to the Corn Market. The carved corner post was given to Derby Museum on demolition.

St James' Lane seen from the end of Victoria Street in about 1866. The bridge in the centre at that time crossed Markeaton Brook which was covered over in 1878 and became The Strand. The Lane was widened to become the present St James' Street and the house on the right was later to be replaced by the post office.

The same view in about 1900, now unrecognizable following the covering of Markeaton Brook to form The Strand, the widening of St James' Lane to form St James' Street, and the construction of a whole new group of buildings.

St Peter's Street in about 1905 showing new buildings on the right hand side, starting with the Midland Drapery.

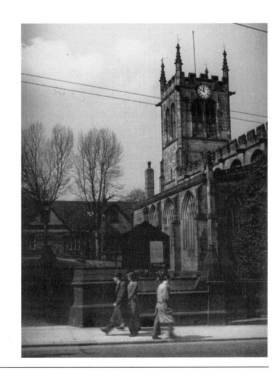

St Peter's church and churchyard, *c*. 1948.

This crowd in St Peter's Street was watching the flood waters rising in the Corn Market and Victoria Street in the great Derby floods of 1932.

Osmaston Road from The Spot in the late 1930s.

It's those floods again! These children make light of the mess outside Woolworth's in Victoria Street, 1932.

St Peter's Street before the construction of the building that became the Midland Drapery, *c.* 1882.

The Boots building on the corner of St Peter's Street and East Street at Christmas 1912.

Amen Alley and Full Street corner in 1882. This old house was a religious bookshop and supplied All Saints' church with books.

Iron Gate
and Sadler Gate

Iron Gate from the west front of All Saints' church looking towards the Market Place in about 1860 before the street was widened. Richard Keene took this photograph and his studio was the centre building on the right with a glass roof.

Iron Gate photographed at the same time as the previous picture and a little nearer to the Market Place. The building visible in the centre is Market Head and the opening to Sadler Gate can also be seen just to the right of it.

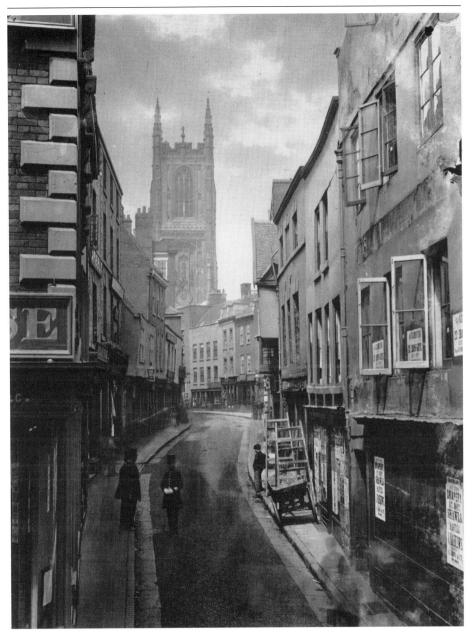

Iron Gate immediately before the widening in 1866. Most of the properties on the right have been purchased and stand empty, awaiting demolition. Every house on this side was removed. The building on the left in the foreground was that of Bemrose the printers.

The widened Iron Gate in 1896.

Sadler Gate in the 1920s.

The Globe Tavern, next to Bemroses in Iron Gate and now known as Mr Jorrocks. In the 1930s it had something of a reputation as a refuge for unsavoury characters.

Queen Street looking towards Iron Gate, past the old Dolphin Inn on the left and All Saints' church, *c.* 1935. Cathedral status was granted on the church in 1927.

All Saints' church seen from St Mary's Gate while undergoing restoration in the early years of the century.

Jack Tasker hand-winding the Cathedral clock in 1954.

The Nottingham Castle Inn in St Michael's Lane, photographed in 1930. Despite its great antiquity and beauty it was demolished in 1962.

Railways

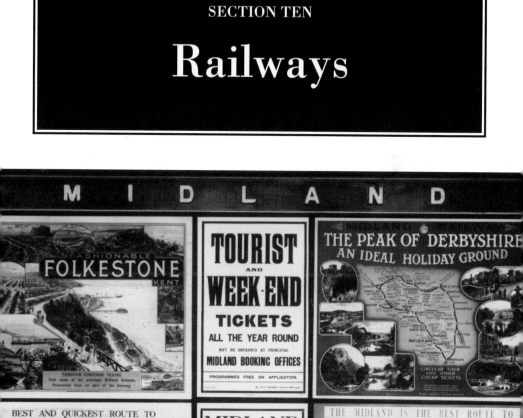

Posters from platform 6 on Derby Midland station, *c.* 1910.

The Midland Railway station in about 1910. The station was originally shared by three railway companies, the North Midland, Midland Counties and Birmingham and Derby Junction Railways, who merged in 1840 to become the Midland Railway. Unfortunately, the original station building was demolished in 1984 and replaced with a modern structure that is sadly out of keeping with its surroundings.

A busy platform at the Midland station in about 1908.

The station was entirely lit by gaslight. A quiet night-time platform 1 is seen here in 1908.

St Mary's goods yard, 'tranship' shed in 1911.

The Midland Railway's Carriage and Waggon Works occupied a large area adjacent to the station. The following sequence of photographs shows the construction of a passenger carriage in 1922: first, preparing the mouldings for the quarterframes.

Assembling quarterframes on the seventh day of work on this carriage.

Contrails fixed and framing almost complete on the tenth day. The total area of the carriage and waggon works in 1873 was fifty acres, and by 1900 it was turning out eight passenger carriages and one hundred and eighty goods waggons per week.

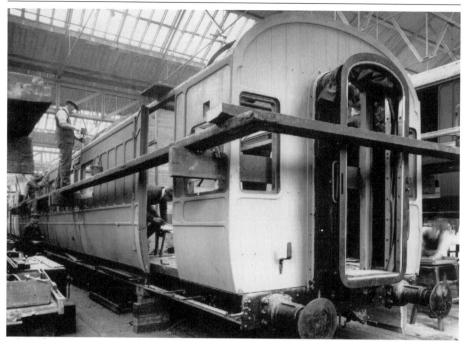

Panels fixed and scaffolding in place for roof fixing on the twenty-fifth day. Total construction time, including interior fittings and painting, was just forty days.

The lifting shop in 1910. A completed seven-compartment, clerestory carriage being lifted onto the bogies.

Platform 2, Midland station lit by gaslight, 1911.

Derby Loco Depot, coal stage with a Cl 4–4–0 taking on water in 1909.

The staff of Joseph Mason Paints celebrate 150 years of the company with a trip to London in 1950. Back row, left to right: Jim Mills (pipe and cap), Ron Warren, Mrs Fleetwood, -?-, Ernie Fleetwood (trilby) and behind, Arthur Lambert, Les Mudd, Mrs Mudd, Albert Book (glasses and hat), Frank Hallsworth, -?-, Mrs Book (partly hidden), Mrs Hallsworth, Tom Hanson, -?-, Mr Franklyn Smith. Fourth row: Reg Scotchbrook, Jim ?, Arthur Radford, Charlie Brown, Mrs Brown, Jim Mills (sen.), Mrs Smith (peeping), Mr Wiltshire (jun.), Eric Wiltshire, Mr E. Ayre (chairman, dark coat and hat), Mrs Ayre, Mrs

Franklyn Smith, Barry Copranak, -?-, Mr Spyby (pipe and hat), -?-. Third row: Mrs Scotchbrook, Wag Thompson (pipe), -?-, -?-, Mrs Snow, Bill Snow, Bill Bousefield, Gordon Warren, Alice Warren (white hat), Fred Barber, Mrs Barber, Albert Potts, Mrs Potts, -?-, -?-. Second row: -?-, -?-, -?-, -?-, Arthur Thompson, -?-, Albert Thompson, Frank Ridgard (glasses), Reg Tomlinson, Wilf Longden, John Smedley (trilby), -?-, Mrs Smedley, -?-, Les Witt (glasses and trilby), Fred Sharman. Front row: Bill Meason, Mrs Thompson, Mrs Longdon, Mrs Tomlinson, George Bacon, Mrs Bacon, Mrs Ayre, -?- (kneeling).

The coppersmith's shop in 1917. The Midland Locomotive Works opened in Derby in 1851 on a site behind the station. Matthew Kirtley was chief engineer. The designs were produced in a large drawing office block and the engines constructed in the workshops.

It has been estimated that in the latter part of the last century the Midland Railway gave employment to about 10,000 people in Derby. This included work generated for allied trades such as the ironfounding industry. The employees of the company had the use of a large Railway Institute built opposite the station in 1882 (and still in existence). This picture shows the institute café, around 1918.

Derby Loco Works wheel shop in 1914.

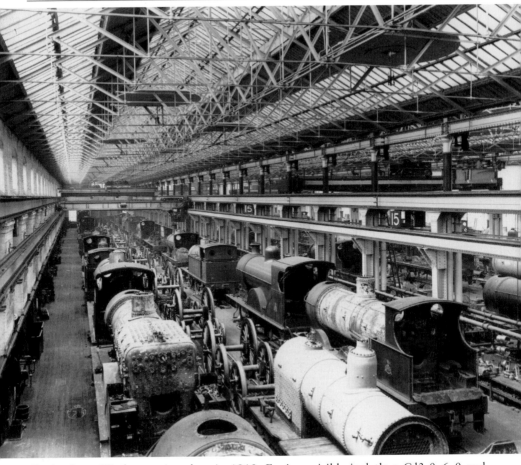

Derby Loco Works erecting shop in 1910. Engines visible include a C13 0–6–0 and C14–4–0 (H boiler). A visitor to these workshops in 1881 wrote, '. . . workshops, flaming with forge-flares, and noisy with ringing hammers: where tools of every descriptrion operate upon metal of every kind; where locomotives that are miracles of mechanism, are fashioned by the Titans of toil. . .'.

The Great Northern Railway Company joined the Midland in Derby following an Act of Parliament in 1872 and the station in Friar Gate was opened in 1878. Arrival of the 'Northern' did not meet with general approval at first because of the amount of destruction wrought in gaining access to a site quite close to the centre of town. This decorative bridge spanning Friar Gate was built by Andrew Handyside and, although now preserved, it was deplored at the time because it replaced some fine Georgian buildings and the Old White Horse Inn. The station closed in 1964.

Friar Gate station in 1938 and a party from John Smith and Sons, the clockmakers, set off for a trip to Skegness. About half of those in the group can be named: extreme left, Ralph Policott, on his left, Harry Farnsworth, in front of the carriage window, Chris Newton, on *his* left, peering from the back, Ned Bucknall. In the centre, hold-

ing hat and coat is Frank Hitchcock, Alf Jordan looks over his shoulder. At the extreme right, front is Alan Smith, behind and to his left is Harold Lane and on his right is Ernest Gilbert with his wife, Lillian and son Alan. A head above them all at the back is Billy Hurd.

THE DERBY RAM

As I was going to Darby, Sir,
  All on a market day,
I met the finest Ram, Sir,
  That ever was fed on hay.
    Daddle-i-day, daddle-i-day,
    Fal-de-ral, fal-de-ral, daddle-i-day.

This Ram was fat behind, Sir,
  This Ram was fat before,
This Ram was ten yards high, Sir,
  Indeed he was no more.
    Daddle-i-day, &c.

The Wool upon his back, Sir,
  Reached up unto the sky,
The Eagles made their nests there, Sir,
  For I heard the young ones cry.
    Daddle-i-day, &c.

The Wool upon his belly, Sir,
  It dragged upon the ground,
It was sold in Darby town, Sir,
  For forty thousand pound.
    Daddle-i-day, &c.

The space between the horns, Sir,
  Was as far as a man could reach,
And there they built a pulpit
  For the Parson there to preach.
    Daddle-i-day, &c.

The teeth that were in his mouth, Sir,
  Were like a regiment of men;
And the tongue that hung between them, Sir,
  Would have dined them twice and again.
    Daddle-i-day, &c.

This Ram jumped o'er the wall, Sir,
  His tail caught on a briar,
It reached from Darby town, Sir,
  All into Leicestershire.
    Daddle-i-day, &c.

And of this tail so long, Sir,
   'Twas ten miles and an ell,
They made a goodly rope, Sir,
   To toll the market bell.
     Daddle-i-day, &c.

This Ram had four legs to walk on, Sir,
   This Ram had four legs to stand,
And every leg he had, Sir,
   Stood on an acre of land.
     Daddle-i-day, &c.

The Butcher that killed this Ram, Sir,
   Was drownded in the blood,
And the boy that held the pail, Sir,
   Was carried away in the flood.
     Daddle-i-day, &c.

All the maids in Darby, Sir,
   Came begging for his horns,
To take them to coopers,
   To make them milking gawns.
     Daddle-i-day, &c.

The little boys of Darby, Sir,
   They came to beg his eyes,
To kick about the streets, Sir,
   For they were football size.
     Daddle-i-day, &c.

The tanner that tanned its hide, Sir,
   Would never be poor any more,
For when he had tanned and retched it,
   It covered all Sinfin Moor.
     Daddle-i-day, &c.

The Jaws that were in his head, Sir,
   They were so fine and thin,
They were sold to a Methodist Parson,
   For a pulpit to preach in.
     Daddle-i-day, &c.

Indeed, Sir, this is true, Sir,
   I never was taught to lie,
And had you been to Darby, Sir,
   You'd have seen it as well as I,
     Daddle-i-day, daddle-i-day,
     Fal-de-ral, fal-de-ral, daddle-i-day.

Acknowledgements

Compiling a collection of photographs like this one depends very much on the generosity and interest of lots of people. I should like to thank all those who have given help either by loaning photographs or books or who have provided information about old Derby. In particular I wish to thank the following:

Aiton & Co. Ltd • Bob Ball • Raymond and Barbara Buxton • Alan Champion
Eric Chapman • Maxwell Craven • *Derby Evening Telegraph* • Derby Museum
Derbyshire Library Service • Richard and Peggy Eyre • Felix Buses
Joyce Harrison • Mr J. Owen Jones
Local Studies Libraries at Derby and Matlock • Joseph Mason Paints
National Railway Museum • Ray Rippingale • Rolls-Royce plc
Royal Crown Derby • Smith of Derby • Les Taylor • Trent Buses

Derbyshire Library Service maintains a large collection of photographic material relating to the county which is held in the Local Studies Libraries at Derby and the Library Headquarters at Matlock. If you have any old photographs of the county which you would be prepared to donate or to lend for copying by the Library Service your local library would be pleased to see them.